THE WHITE EAGLE INHERITANCE

Describes how the Lodge was founded, the identity and mission of White Eagle himself and the principal features of the Lodge's teaching.

Contents

The Principles of the White Eagle Lodge

The Lodge teaches:

1. that God, the Eternal Spirit, is both Father and Mother;
2. that the Son, the Cosmic Christ, is also the light which shines in the human heart. By reason of this divine sonship, all are brothers and sisters in spirit, a brotherhood which embraces all life visible and invisible, including the fairy and angelic kingdoms·
3. the expression of these principles in daily life, through service;
4. the awareness of the invisible world, which bridges separation and death and reveals the eternal unity of life;
5. that life is governed by five cosmic laws, namely: reincarnation, cause and effect, opportunity, correspondences, compensation (equilibrium and balance);
6. that the ultimate goal of mankind is that the inner light should become so strong and radiant that even the cells of the physical body are transmuted into finer substances which can overcome mortality. This is known as the Christing of man, or — in the words of the ancient Brotherhood — the blooming of the Rose on the Cross of matter.

Foreword

If anyone is well qualified to write about White Eagle's teaching and the work of the White Eagle Lodge, that person is Ingrid Lind. She and her family have worked closely with us for about thirty years, and for much of this time she personally led an associated group at Chinnor, whose members met regularly to study and discuss the teaching, to learn about meditation and also to take part in the healing work.

Well known and loved in the astrological world, where she was vice-principal of the Faculty of Astrological Studies and vice-president of the Astrological Association — and is now patron of both — Ingrid is also the author of the popular and most valuable book *Astrologically Speaking*, in which she gives an account of her many years' work as an astrological consultant. Many friends and members of the White Eagle Lodge were first introduced to the teaching through a consultation with Ingrid.

We are grateful to her for her willing acceptance of the challenge of writing another book at a time when she had been hoping to sit back and enjoy her years of retirement. This is typical of her staunch support of White Eagle's work throughout the years, and we do hope that now she really will be able to relax and enjoy the fruits of her labours. We wish her success with her books and hope that she will have many years of peace and happiness both in the heart of her family and in joining quietly in our work at the White Temple.

JOAN G. HODGSON

Introduction

First, let me say what a privilege it is to have been asked to write this book. It will be difficult to do justice to a community I hold in such respect and affection.

It was in 1947, when Ronald Fraser and I were in Paris, that we first heard about the White Eagle Lodge. This was through an old friend of mine, Betty Simpson, who had taught me dancing at the Margaret Morris School in Chelsea in the late 1920s. While visiting Paris she told me that she and her partner had both become members of a White Eagle Lodge in Edinburgh; and she so impressed us that when I was seriously ill with heart trouble in 1950 she easily persuaded me to write to the healing secretary for absent healing. Although I had been out of hospital for some weeks, fever recurred if I left my bed.

The charming, friendly letter I got back made me sure that one day I would go to the Lodge, and I recalled an out-of-the-body experience which has a close enough connection with the Lodge's history to warrant its telling. This had taken place in May 1940, in Suffolk, where I was staying with my sister and brother-in-law. I think of it as a 'Samuel and Eli' experience, because it started in a similar way. I was lying in bed, nearly asleep, when a voice called me quite loudly and I jumped out of bed, supposing it to be that of my brother-in-law; but no one was awake, so I went back. The same thing happened for three successive nights, and the third time I replied, feeling rather foolish, 'Speak, Lord, for thy servant heareth' (1 Samuel 3.2-9). Then I put my head back on the pillow and went to sleep. The next thing I knew was that I was awake in full, enchanted consciousness. The room was filled with a light that came from a figure that was sitting on my bed and chatting to me. There was no sense of surprise or shock. The speaker was in mid-sentence and I 'clocked in', as it were, to a state of remembering during a certain part of his discourse. There were no hellos or goodbyes; rather it was I who arrived and departed, gained and then lost consciousness of the scene.

What did he look like? He was perfectly real, clear and solid. He had dark hair and wore a white robe-like garment. Vaguely I remember a kindly, bearded face and the deep sense of comfort and affection which enveloped me. Yet his words and the light which filled the room were the vivid part of the experience, and it is the reality — the voice — that I recall, together with the urgency to remember what was said more than what was seen.

What did he say? His message was personal and concerned what I must do. As near as I can recall, it ran: 'You are reading widely and finding out about things.' This was true. I had begun taking books out of libraries and was deep in the writings of Steiner, Evelyn, Underhill and others. 'This is right,' said my visitor. 'Go on reading. We do not wish you to join any group. When the time is right for this, you will know beyond a shadow of doubt.' The vision did not fade away; it was I who faded back into sleep and awoke next morning with a memory that has never left me and is of that *rare dream* quality that does not lose its impact. It was a friendly, loving contact, and the comfort it provided was immense: not least important was the assurance it gave that other-worldly beings were able to communicate if they so wished.

The receiving of healing from the White Eagle Lodge does not entail membership. Their healing certainly worked in my case. Slowly but surely the following year I was able to be up and about, although for almost twelve months I was pushed around in a wheelchair. We did not live in England again until 1951, when Ronald said: 'We should go to that Lodge place and thank them for your healing.' So we made an appointment to see Joan Hodgson, then healing secretary. As we were leaving St Mary Abbots Place, which was then the headquarters, Ronald remarked what an impressive person she was. He said that he had a feeling we should go there again and that perhaps it could be *the place*. As I had felt exactly the same, I agreed and said I would attend a service there in the New Year.

While living in Paris we had read a great deal on the subject of mysticism, and Ronald was very impressed on reading the

White Eagle books that these seemed to sum up the ancient wisdom (see page 27) that tallied with our own basic beliefs.[1] Thus it happened, and we were sure 'beyond a shadow of doubt' that this was where our work lay. When eventually I told the leader of the Lodge of my experience of the apparition, she said, very calmly: 'Yes, dear. That was the Master R.' (See Chapter 1.) Often when a person is told something stupendous, he is unable to take it in. However, one thing led to another, and in 1953 we went on our first retreat to New Lands, the country house which is the present Lodge headquarters. By this time we were both feeling that when the time seemed ripe we would apply to be initiated into the Brotherhood; we were convinced that this was the path for us. Ronald, now over sixty and retired, had never been a keen joiner of groups, still less of unorthodox religious communities. His knighthood had been earned by his rank in the foreign service, and he had previously spent some years at the Board of Trade. The author of well over thirty books, he was so compulsive a writer that while living in a small house during the war he had written for an hour each morning in a henhouse. I only wish I had such energy now! We were initiated in June 1954, and from that moment until Ronald's death twenty years later it was White Eagle's teaching that meant everything to him. Though he was unable in his later years to travel to attend meetings of the Brotherhood, I took it to his bedside until the very week he died.

I mention him largely because it may be of interest, to fellow scholars of mysticism and those with keenly critical minds, to learn that the Lodge does not appeal only to elderly ladies. Independence was strong in him, and while approving of vegetarianism, he maintained that ham was a legitimate part of salad! Similarly, as he had had a moderate-sized drink every night for many years, something tells me that nothing interfered with this habit. Excess was not in his nature, but humour most definitely was, and one of the things that appealed most to him about White Eagle was that he could be amusing. When I stayed with my friend Cynthia, the Lady Sandys, who channels Ronald's spirit very easily, I had only recently been asked by the Lodge to write this book and told her I was somewhat nervous about doing it. He immediately took the matter up, and I quote: 'Now, my dearest, you are undertaking a most important work — the writing of the history and work of the White Eagle Lodge. It is quite natural that they should choose you. Your book on astrology is very readable, and they need a running, easy style to interest everyone — no church language. You've no need to be afraid. You know your stuff, and we shall all be at your elbow, including White Eagle himself and both founders, and all who have passed over are anxious that a book should be written for everyman. I shall delight in helping you. Alice Bailey is here with me now. She is laughing and saying you must put in all the funny bits and the human sayings of White Eagle that will suit the fringe readers and those who read only out of curiosity.'

Well, of course, this cheered me no end. But while I remember laughing many times, it is quite another thing to remember exactly why. It is certain, though, that laughter is very much a part of life on the other side.

1. The History

The Story of the Oracle

Most children have times of loneliness or fear, but few are fortunate enough to have a teacher and mentor as loving and wise as White Eagle. Grace Cooke, as she became known to so many in later life as a medium, had another name, given to her by her spirit guide White Eagle in early days. From now on I shall refer to her as Minesta. It means 'mother', and is indeed most appropriate to one who during her lifetime became a friend, counsellor and 'mother' to thousands. Although at the present stage of the White Eagle Lodge its members are not officially spiritualists, it is a fact that Minesta conducted services and gave clairvoyance on behalf of spiritualism, spreading the conviction of the after-death state and bringing its comfort to an enormous number of people for over twenty years. This lengthy period of hard work and endurance was necessary in order to toughen and at the same time refine her character; meanwhile, her sensitivity increased. At the end of this twenty-year period, Minesta, now in early middle age, was married with a home and two children to care for. She went several times a week to an important centre of the spiritualist movement in London, the Stead Borderland Library, where a considerable effort was often needed in order to help bereaved persons rise out of their despair.

It was at this time that Sir Arthur Conan Doyle opened his Psychic Bookshop in Victoria Street, and gradually a friendship arose between Minesta and Sir Arthur's daughter, Mary Conan Doyle, who ran it. On hearing about White Eagle, Sir Arthur — now, in 1930, a sick man — was greatly looking forward to meeting Minesta. They never met, for he died in July that same year, but it is significant in view of later events that their similar interests had drawn them together before his passing. All this leads naturally to the story of the Hermit of Bagnaia, which was first related in the Paris *Bulletin des Polaires* of 9 June 1930. The full translation appears in the fourth chapter of the White Eagle publication *The Return of Arthur Conan Doyle*, which I now give in summary.[1]

In 1908 a young man holidaying in Viterbo, near Rome, noticed an impressive, monkish individual called Father Julian to whom he felt greatly drawn. The old man lived in a ruined hut, surviving on what he could find to eat, and was never seen to go near a church. The local people wished him to leave. The young man tried to persuade him to take money, clothing and a better shelter, but the hermit assured him that he needed nothing and had to stay there in spite of hostility until the day came for him to embark on a long, long journey. The young man visited him daily and listened to words of goodness, true love and brotherhood. Although firmly attached to the things of the world, he recognized an initiate and respected his firm resolve to refuse all aid. One day he found Father Julian unconscious from a deep wound in the leg. He helped the old man to his shelter, dressed the wound, and found to his surprise that in only three days the wound was completely healed. What mysterious herbs had been used? The boy, by now accustomed to his questions being ignored, did not enquire.

At the end of his holiday the youth made his way sadly to the hut for the last time. What the old man whispered to the lad he now called 'his son' will never be known, but in his last moments handed him some sheets of paper which were 'a small fragment from the Book of the Science of Life and of Death'. The recipient of these pages never forgot the last words spoken to him:

> Should you at any time require help or counsel you have only to follow the instructions which are contained in this old manuscript — *you will receive your reply*. It may even occur one day that *I myself will reply to you*. But remember never to divulge to anyone in the world what is written on these pages, for in doing so you run the risk for yourself, as well as for the one who obtains knowledge, of madness or death.

It was two years later, and in great mental distress, that the young man consulted the manuscript and made use of the prescribed arithmetical calculations. The reply showed itself to be astonishingly correct and to contain great wisdom. Only then did he speak to a group of his friends who were students of the esoteric and did groups come into being. In 1923, Father Julian kept his promise and replied personally. In April 1930, by means of the 'oracle de la force astrale' he sent his last message 'to his well-beloved sons': 'And now the Lord Buddha has opened to him the Path of Light'. Here we come to the end of what we know. It could only be operated by someone with the necessary soul vibration, which is no doubt why the youth was brought to Father Julian. The intuition of the operator of the 'oracle de la force astrale' was doubtless an important factor when it came to sending or receiving messages. Having fulfilled its appointed purpose, this oracle has now ceased to exist.

The Polaire Brethren
The next phase in the story was when the instruction came for the two main operators to go to Paris and establish a group which was to be called the Polaire Brotherhood, after the French name for the pole star — the star which helps all men to find the way. Arriving as near-penniless strangers, they were helped until soon the Brotherhood occupied handsome premises on the slopes of Montmartre. Their monthly magazine, the *Bulletin des Polaires*, gradually reached a circulation of ten thousand. World War I had only just come to an end, and it was disconcerting to be told of forthcoming 'years of fire' even more destructive than the ones just experienced. No further messages came from Father Julian, but members and friends of the White Eagle Lodge will consider it important to know that the 'force astrale' was now under the guidance of the Wise Knight or Chevalier Rose-Croix (see page 56). This leader was later found to be the Master R., whom many also know as the Rosicrucian brother Francis Bacon. Those readers who have had the good fortune to see a Master will agree with a visitor from India who, when asked what a particular Master was like, answered, 'He is all love'. This is the keynote of a Master or initiate: the projection of Light or ray of Love. This projection of Love or Light forms the basis for the dedicated work of the Brothers of the White Eagle Lodge.

But, you may well ask, what has 'all this Polaire Brethren stuff' got to do with Minesta? In the answer to this lies what is, to my mind, the most convincing proof that the power of the Spirit has been directly responsible for the formation of the White Eagle Lodge. It appears that after his death Sir Arthur sought our Sages, who enabled him to transmit a long message through the 'force astrale' with the aid of Master R. Sir Arthur had found that much of what he had told spiritualists about life in the next world needed revision. This new information could not, it seems, at that moment be conveyed through the 'force astrale', but this French brotherhood sent one of their members to England to see Lady Conan Doyle, who would introduce him to the medium chosen by the Master R. for the purpose of channelling this message. The chosen Polaire Brother would recognize her at once, and there should be no delay. Who was this chosen medium? It was Minesta.

The first message from Sir Arthur — to whom we shall now refer, for the sake of convenience, as A.C.D. — came on 27 January 1931 and on what was in fact the first occasion that a Polaire Brother had met Minesta. A.C.D. told her that he knew her from a life long ago in ancient Egypt. The Brother gave her a little star which he pinned on her dress with a gesture of blessing and protection. In the months that followed, both Minesta and her husband, Ivan Cooke, wore little six-pointed Polaire stars, and both were sensitive enough to be receptive to the Polaire ray. They had been picked out, as it were, by a spotlight which was to be a very helpful influence. Yet even A.C.D. had to wait until he had experienced a wide range of the heavenly kingdom before giving his full message. Those unused to 'spirit communications' may be interested to learn how soon after death the soul of one who has passed over can be seen by a sensitive. Ten days after his passing, A.C.D. joined his family in a welcome to Minesta, although she alone could *see* him. That same evening, with White Eagle acting as spokesman, a Conan Doyle family reunion took place. It is presumed that White Eagle co-operated very closely in this contact, for Minesta entered a deep, trance-like state similar to the sleep of a child. In the many years that followed, this was how White Eagle spoke through her. No one could doubt that a member of the opposite sex was speaking: her voice deepened, and the delivery and choice of words was certainly not her own. White Eagle played a major part in the transmission of the earlier A.C.D. messages. It is interesting to note that A.C.D.'s mannerisms and habitual terms of expression still crept in, though Minesta had never met him during his time on earth.

The link with the Polaire Brethren continued, and later that year a message came from the Sages in Tibet concerning a treasure that was to be found in the Pyrenees. The nature of the treasure was unspecified, but the Brethren were told to ask Minesta to accompany the party. In spite of being told it would be a dangerous expedition, she agreed to go and was accompanied by her husband. The Polaires' message was that on the third day of the quest Minesta would be the one to find the treasure; it was not said that the party as a whole would find it. Sure enough, something of the utmost importance to Minesta occurred on that very day. In the heights, near the Castle of Monségur, she suddenly saw walking towards her a shining figure who approached her very naturally and talked in the friendliest way. She knew without a doubt that here was one who belonged, as she herself put it, 'to the Sphere of St John'; and from that moment she acquired a radiance and an inner happiness which gave her the impetus to start the work of the Star Brotherhood (see page 53).

It was at Burstow Manor in Surrey that, under White Eagle's direction, a chapel was created in which the first White Eagle Brothers were initiated.

The Link with the Albigenses

Minesta tells the full story of how the community known as the Albigenses had lived in the Pyrenees in order to spread the Light of God. [2] As always where the White Light manifests itself, so also do the forces of the shadow, and in this case, the Albigenses were forced into a cave on the mountain side. The cave was then sealed up and they were left to die. It is believed that no less a person than St John the Divine had originally travelled to the East and formed the Albigensian brotherhood, which only came to the West some centuries later.

Before leaving England, Minesta had been warned, with reference to a cave in the mountains: 'Be careful, for the water rises every twelve hours.' The shining figure now pointed to the very cave she had been shown when in London, with stalactites and stalagmites forming pillars and, at the far end, a reredos and altar carved out of the natural rock. When the party visited the site they heard the sound of rushing water as the cavern filled up; the words spoken in the vision were thus substantiated. Minesta did not fail to put mental questions about the treasure to her visitor. That there was a treasure he did not deny, but the message he gave was that the world's standard of values must be changed before man could be entrusted with the use of precious metals and stones. Until humanity was ready to use nature's wealth for the spiritual culture of the whole community, this wealth would not bring joy so much as a heavy burden. Man must learn the correct value to the soul of both spiritual and material gifts before he can handle either safely and happily. Only through the development of soul knowledge and its use for the good of all would humanity qualify to find the buried treasure. It therefore seemed that the first step towards the locating of this treasure was to find some spiritual clue which would help towards the completion of this task.

The message also stated that in the life and teachings of Jesus, the Christ, would be found the key to the spiritual nature buried within man. After the Resurrection and departure of his Master, John the beloved disciple voyaged to the West and visited this same mountain, where he spent long hours in spiritual communion with the Master. Then, returning to the East, John founded the brotherhood known as the Albigenses, sharing with its members the wisdom he had learnt. Its treasure and its secret might be called the complete Gospel of St John, of which the existing Gospel is but a fragment. Before his passing, John had been called to the Sages in the East, where he spent the last years of his life. He did not die as most men do, but rose into the higher life as his Master had done before him. Centuries later, the Albigenses sailed to the West, to the Pyrenees. They were still known as the Brethren of John, whose Gospel was their secret and treasure.

Within a year or two of Minesta's Pyrenean journey, directions were received to form a group in England of the White Brotherhood (see page 53) whose first task was to help humanity through what were to be 'years of fire'. Thus it was the very same sages who had produced the oracle who now arranged for the reception of the long series of later messages and the teaching which, it is hoped, will lead man from ignorance into the Eternal Light. Through Minesta, more became known of the Brothers of the Unseen, the White Brethren, who say they come from the cave of the 'cross within the circle' in the Far East. The Albigenses had also taken this as their symbol, and it denotes them as 'those who have overcome the darkness of the lower self and by precept and practice been admitted into the holy rites of brotherhood and continue to partake of holy communion with their Master throughout their lives and live as brothers in service to mankind'. Continued communion through brotherly service is symbolized by the tau cross, which is, however, incomplete without its surrounding circle of white light.

Minesta tells how, from the day of her return, her work concentrated largely on the teaching of St John. When the oracle had ceased to function, instructions from the sages came to her direct from White Eagle himself. She was helped to found a brotherhood not unlike, she hoped and believed, that first brotherhood of John, and a 'Church of St John' in which the Johannine teaching could be lived and practised — namely the White Eagle Lodge. During the years of World War II, the 'years of fire' which had been predicted, messages were received for the book *The Living Word of the Gospel of St John*. It was published in the earnest hope that every reader should understand that its message comes from the invisible Powers who planned it long ago. It recent years it has been reprinted and revised for the present day and the world's entry into the New Age, and it is now entitled *The Living Word of St John* by White Eagle.[3] The emblem of St John is the white eagle. In her lifetime, modesty would have forbidden Grace Cooke (Minesta) to claim that this book was the transcription — dare I say it? — of messages given directly by John in order to clarify his own Gospel. We are confident that this is the treasure.

The Founding of the Lodge

It is often remarked that the White Eagle Lodge is very much a family affair. It was in 1935, and on the direct instruction of White Eagle himself, that this became so. Ten or so years earlier a small group had formed in Middlesex and differences had arisen when certain committee members wanted the teaching to concentrate solely on evidence of survival of death, while others wanted there to be a greater focus on White Eagle's message. This had eventually caused the Lodge's move to Burstow Manor in Surrey, where the Cooke family's life's work really started. Minesta's two daughters, Joan and Ylana, were now old enough to work; and while Joan had trained as a teacher, White Eagle suggested that Ylana should train as a secretary and also run Burstow as a healing home. She had to take down his many addresses, given at spiritualist centres, as the tape recorder had not yet been invented. When the lease of Burstow expired, White Eagle made it clear that the work had to be transferred to London. This was in 1935, and he said that by operating as a united family the Lodge could operate through the difficult times that lay ahead. Received after the 'years of fire' prediction, this message seems, on looking back, to have presaged World War II; yet when war was declared in September 1939 it still came as a shock. White Eagle's instruction to his followers that they should project the picture of peace into the work had been mistakenly interpreted as a prophecy of world peace.

A further shock occurred when Pembroke Hall, the first London lodge, was wrecked by a bomb. But those who felt that a true centre of Light should be protected were told they must learn to share the fate of humanity if they were to be able to help and understand others in times of need — why should they expect to escape the common lot? It also came as a surprise to be told to find a new centre in London, and that Minesta would recognize the right place as soon as she entered it. The 'family' set forth complete with Joan, who gave up her teaching to help in the finding and settling into the new home of the Lodge. The day, with continual air raids, was unpropitious, but when Minesta entered the courtyard of 9 St Mary Abbots Place, she said instantly: 'This is the place. I shall work here.'

While the lease was being negotiated, the salvage work went on round the corner at Pembroke Hall. The furnishings really did seem to have been protected: two altar vases are in use to this day. These had been blown right across the hall, and it must have been Ivan Cooke — a splendid carver — who saw to the reassembly of the then shattered carving of the white eagle which still hangs above the altar. Nearly two hundred chairs, curtains and carpets were saved and kindly stored by the friends who had put the family up since four days before the bombing occurred. The fact that they received this warning from the spirit powers seems a very adequate answer to any who complained that the place should have been protected. Disaster, though narrowly averted when fire bombs fell in plenty, did not reoccur, and work still continues in the same premises to the present day; St Mary Abbots Place remains the home of the London Lodge.

2. The Teaching

Teaching from Discarnate Sources
As all of White Eagle's teaching comes under this heading, it is appropriate that I should write something about what could be called an unorthodox source. It is high time that it was recognized that there are many who live in a state of consciousness more subtle than that which is implied when we say we are 'conscious'. It ought to be widely known that 'seeing' is a genuine operation of the psyche and yields genuine information about worlds other than our familiar physical one. Such sensitives make use of mechanisms which are not open to surgical investigation but are capable of being investigated by clairvoyants. It is the spiritual world that we should call the 'real' world. When it becomes reality for us it can convey systematic and continuous instruction that can lead us, in time, to the metamorphosis of our personal selves into our subtle selves.

The basic theme is that mankind has all knowledge within himself. You or I, though nothing and nobody as such, are in reality Light. Knowledge or reality are accessible through a technique of imaginative meditation, by which we mean an identification of ourselves with the creative consciousness. Consciously or subconsciously, every soul has but one right and duty: to become one with the higher consciousness that projected it. We should constantly feel at one with the Star that shines in our own hearts and say: 'I am That; That am I. I am the Resurrection and the Life.'

Nothing is much good until we find it out for ourselves — but how? The path of discovery is meditation, and the first find is the Light or the six-pointed Star in our own hearts. We must be able to say 'I am the flame', and this must become a fact, part of our conscious experience. This may seem a rather vague and unhelpful way of living; but in fact there is no way in which you can exercise greater power and align yourself with the Supreme Will more effectively. It is this sort of prayer, meditation and unremitting thought that will bring satisfaction to the countless millions who have an unfulfilled awareness that they should be 'doing something — but what?' The White Eagle Lodge tries to give the answer.

The Light itself cannot fail to help. This is the light and warmth that is brought to us by those who offer help and friendliness in whatever form; the Light that pours through the human heart.

Who is White Eagle?

Many readers will be familiar with the leaflet written by Grace Cooke (Minesta) and distributed by the White Eagle Publishing Trust. [1] I am making free use of this and of material found in other Lodge literature. Minesta wrote that 'White Eagle' is the name given to the personality, now known to thousands throughout the world, who spoke through her from the early 1930s until her death in 1979, using her voice to give his messages and teachings.

He was never known to speak harshly or unkindly, to judge or condemn, to be fearful or pessimistic. He was always to be hopeful, gentle and loving. He always spoke with conviction, with quiet authority and with a deep understanding of the needs of humanity. The depth and quality of his wisdom and knowledge proves that these came from a spiritually developed and highly evolved being. He himself would make no such claim, for he is the embodiment of simplicity, gentleness and humility, and repeated constantly that he was merely an instrument: 'Only God is good and He it is that doeth the work.'

His messages, consistent throughout, came through for those forty-five years, and outlined a whole way of life. Those who follow it find it leads to happiness, health and fulfilment. It is worth remembering that all fresh revelations throughout the ages have been transmitted through the visions or inspirations of men and women chosen for such a purpose. When asked how he was able to use the vocal organs of a human instrument, White Eagle replied:

The human instrument I use was related to me in past incarnations. She has been trained through many lives to become my mouthpiece. There is complete harmony and at-one-ment between us (the operator and the instrument). When a communication is to be made we draw close to her and speak into a golden disc of light we can see at the back of the head. It can be likened to an etheric microphone, built of substance extracted from the human soul and the physical nervous system. It is a finer form of matter, or in other words, matter of higher frequency than physical matter, therefore unseen by earthly people. When we desire to speak we approach very close to the human instrument we are going to use and concentrate our thoughts on this golden disc, and transform our thoughts into words which are spoken through the voice of the human instrument. You tell us that this voice, when recorded on a tape or disc, convincingly registers as an other-worldly personality.

I would confirm this. The first time I heard Minesta in trance, I was impressed how neatly she accomplished it. (Some mediums make such a fuss! I nearly said 'They grunt and groan', which would be unkind, so I'll pretend I never thought that.)

The name 'White Eagle', which seems to irritate those who think that foreign names are chosen by 'all mediums', means in American Indian legend, 'spiritual teacher'. The white eagle flies straight towards the sun; in the ancient mysteries, too, the white eagle symbolized the higher powers of man or one who could work with clear vision in the secret or inner worlds. Most important of all, a white eagle is the symbol of St John, in whose Gospel lies hidden the story of how man can develop through brotherhood and illumination. Further details of White Eagle's previous lives are provided by Minesta. An incarnation as a Mayan chieftain is written of in her book *The Illuminated Ones*; at that time he was a 'plumed serpent' or initiate of the ancient wisdom (see next section). [2] He also had an incarnation in France as member of a brotherhood which used the symbol of the six-pointed star. There was a life in Greece as a teacher and philosopher; and he was known to many also as a Tibetan, an Egyptian priest-pharaoh, even as a brother in some obscure order and as a medieval alchemist. But in whatever bodies or personalities he was known or unknown to her personally, to her he remained always 'dear old White Eagle' who had loved and cared for her from her earliest childhood.

I shall try in further pages to summarize some of the teachings. I would advise those seeking a deeper understanding to study the many books now available through the Publishing Trust at New Lands. I know White Eagle would want it stressed that his teachings come through him as spokesman for a group of White Brothers (I hasten to add that in these days of touchiness over racialism we now say 'Star Brotherhood', so that there is no possibility of 'white' being taken to refer to the colour of one's skin). Books containing these are read in every English-speaking country, and the booklist contains details of translations. Their wide appeal lies in the fact that answers are provided for many seemingly unanswerable problems concerning life here — White Eagle's teachings apply to everyday living — and in the hereafter.

I will try to show how applicable this teaching is to the present new age of Aquarius and will repeat now that belief is in the eternal or Christ spirit, the 'Son of God, not only as a personality but as the light which should be the activating force or will to good in the heart of everyone'. Here we need to differentiate between Christ the Son of God or Cosmic Christ and the historical Jesus the Galilean. White Eagle teaches that the ultimate goal of every man is to develop the light of the Christ spark within his heart. We are told that this is a continuous process and that man lives not once but many times on earth before he can become 'man made perfect'. Hand in hand with the teaching of reincarnation comes the knowledge that the soul survives the death of the body, existing in a higher state of life where it is invisible to mortal sight though capable of being seen by many who possess clearer vision. This knowledge is of comfort both to the bereaved and to those who, on passing over are unable to make themselves seen by their closest contacts. The most important work of the White Eagle Lodge lies in trying to take away the fear of death.

The Ancient or Ageless Wisdom and the Sun-Men
In a very real sense, the whole teaching of the White Eagle Lodge concerns the ancient wisdom which is the basis of all forms of religion. Occult teaching states that this wisdom, which has persisted since the earth came into existence, was brought to the earth by the Sun-Men, souls who have advanced far beyond the comprehension of the most powerful human intelligence. They also teach that these sun-beings have in their charge every cycle of evolving human souls. The ancient wisdom has it that the two

forces of light and darkness both have an important part to play
in the human soul. It is perhaps natural to associate light with
goodness and darkness with evil, yet White Eagle's account of
these two forces is rather different. In *Sun-men of the Americas*,
he says:

> We would draw your attention to the importance of balance. These
> two aspects, light and dark, positive and negative, are working
> together to bring about balance and equilibrium, which is one of
> the fundamental laws of life. The ultimate is absolute balance within
> the microcosm, and within the macrocosm. Thus the two aspects
> of life, good and evil, seen from the higher state of consciousness
> are two forces working together to produce the perfect life, and
> the power of mastership in the individual life. As well as invisible
> presences, invisible beings outside himself, there is also that within
> every man which is both positive and negative, light and dark. What
> must be remembered is that man holds the balance within his own
> heart. It is of vital importance that this balance between the positive
> and negative should be kept. [3]

In ancient wisdom the moon symbolized the soul, that 'deep
inner part of man's being where dwell the memories of past lives,
past thought-habits and past triumphs'. [4] Jenny Dent puts it clearly
in her book for children *Great Teachers*: 'All the world religions
have close links because the truth they contain is a part of the
Ancient Wisdom'. [5] This is a name given to the truths about God
and life which were originally brought to earth many thousands
of years ago by wise spiritual teachers. In short, the ancient wisdom
is the common truth that lies behind all religion. In the White Eagle
Lodge this is expressed through White Eagle's teaching by means
of books; it is learnt through service and prayer and in becoming
part of a world-wide healing mission to humanity.

The Sun Gods were great ones born with a special mission.
Jesus was one of them, and they all came into existence to be
channels for the Lord Christ. The path of initiation can be traced
in the teachings of the four Gospels, which show the training or
unfolding of the soul through matter. These ancient ones were
known in America as 'plumed serpents' because they each
appeared to have grown a crown of feathers, which was actually
a divine fire or illumination, the mark of their spiritual greatness.
Like Jesus, they came to be saviours. I found this information
in early messages from White Eagle, who also said that in a very

early life he had known a Sun God and that his message had been very similar to that of Christ, his earthly existence starting with a miraculous birth and ending in a crucifixion and resurrection.

Markings on ancient stones record their visitations. Advanced clairvoyants can see revealed the beautiful lives lived long ago by the ancient brethren of the Great White Light. The results of such activity can be seen in many parts of the world, including our own. White Eagle says that all truth — all ancient wisdom — lies within our hearts. The *Christos* has come again and again, but He came particularly often in ancient times through the Sun Gods, the truly ancient ones. In this way, the White Brotherhood has always existed: it is an essential part of the cosmos. All down the ages there have been brotherhoods concerned with presenting the esoteric truth to those members of mankind ready to receive it.

The New Age

White Eagle refers to the New or Aquarian Age very specifically as a time when man's intuition or 'the mind in the heart' will be used far more. Indeed, the whole structure of earthly life, of government, education, art, music, literature as well as religion will then be on a spiritual basis. This has been referred to by other groups as 'living in the fourth dimension'. It may be hard to imagine this, but if we really progress towards the use of spiritual healing, which takes account of the soul as well as the body, man will gradually grow in intuition and thus observe the laws of healthy living. This must be so if he is to live on earth in the way that God intended.

At present, nearing the end of the twentieth century, we are all enduring the birth pangs of the New Age. What is happening is a breaking up of old conditions to make way for the new. Outworn creeds and dogmas, outmoded forms of life — all must go, even the old forms of government and religion. The following quotation from the last two pages of the leaflet on the White Brotherhood (or Star Brotherhood, as it is now termed) is so relevant to this subject that it must not be omitted:

> The Brotherhood of the Great Light is coming into full and glorious manifestation again. This will be brought about through a real brotherhood between men and not through books, knowledge or through established churches or religions. It will dawn in the hearts of tried and tested souls initiated into groups of the Star

Brotherhood which will spring up in many places.

Remember always, however, that the origin of this brotherhood of the Great Light so far as this world is concerned was here in Britain. This has not been spoken of before because the time was not ready. Now it is time for you to understand the work now active in your own land, bringing into manifestation from the very soil and stones of your island the true light of spiritual brotherhood — brotherhood in very truth, not in word only, but in life, in service, in kindness and co-operation, in patience, tolerance and love. Thus will brotherhood grow in strength.

It is noticeable how frequently the mountain top is referred to in connection with the masters, with groups and lodges. Think about this. On the mountain top is stillness and peace. So when you want to get beyond the turmoil of everyday thought, you naturally aspire to the heights. You think of the centre of holiness as on a mountain. Actually what happens is a raising of consciousness to a plane above the material, above the world of darkness. The earth plane is a plane of darkness, and the earth planet is the darkest planet; but even the darkest planet can become light. The day will come when, through the efforts of humanity, the very particles, the atoms of the earth will change and evolve into a state of light and beauty, an ethereal state in which the earth, like other planets unknown to men, will become invisible to young souls on other planets, in the far, far distant future.

What we tell you is true. The brethren of the Star work to help you. They are ever with you. They turn your thoughts upward. Seek first the kingdom; seek first the contact with the infinite, the realization of the Presence. [6]

It seems to be said by all who have higher knowledge that mankind as a whole has passed through the lowest point of its evolutionary cycle and is now advancing towards an age of harmony when the whole earth will become etherialized and more beautiful. In Joan Hodgson's book *Why On Earth?* she tells us that the time is coming when twin souls will more frequently be allowed the joy of working together in human marriage. [7] But their lives must be devoted to the service of humanity so that their united love becomes a beacon flame to warm and inspire everything in their environment.

All these things will occur in the Age of Aquarius which is starting now. It will bring an ever-deepening understanding of the meaning of brotherhood between men and nations; and as more advanced souls come into incarnation, more marriages of this kind will bless humanity and speed up the evolution of the whole race. Jesus said, 'No man putteth new wine into old bottles', and change must take place in order to make way for the New Age. New religious concepts and forms will certainly be needed.

As far as White Eagle's teaching of the Father-Mother God is concerned, it is interesting to see how at the present time, an awareness of the feminine or mother principle is growing. The women's liberation movement has sprung up relatively recently, and confusion still exists concerning the father and mother principles and also the nature and function of spirit and soul in man. When spirit comes down to dwell in flesh, it creates the soul; the soul then becomes that part of our being which is subsequently built up by the various experiences received during successive incarnations. But perhaps I should explain why the soul is described as the feminine aspect of our lives, the mother principle. In esoteric teaching, one finds the soul representing the mother, the feminine or second principle of life. There is no doubt that the father or masculine side is the first principle. Genesis tells us how the woman was taken from the 'rib' or heart of Adam, who needed this second aspect in order to be complete. Soul has to do with feeling. It gives feeling to the self of man and is the intuitive part of him. The soul of the world is made up of the feeling of the world, while that of a nation is seen in the feeling of the people of that nation. The New or Aquarian Age will bring the 'mother' or 'woman' aspect of life into greater prominence; it will usher in greater intuition and an increase in the soul power of mankind. Not until the first principle which represents the father (will) is perfectly balanced by the second or mother principle (intuition) will the Christ child be brought forth as the perfect outcome of their union.

It should nevertheless be understood that a perfect blending of male and female is what should be striven for within each individual man and woman, for each of us contains both qualities. In one life a person may have the male predominant; in another, the female. Certain basic qualities are reflected in each of us by the Trinity. There is no individual who cannot, in due time, become Christed. God created man a living soul, but this soul is not necessarily immortal; it is not the eternal part of man. The soul's body could be described as a fine replica of the physical form. This soul-body is the bridge between earth and heaven for an incarnate human being. Hopefully, having learnt that there is a 'mind in the heart', man will in this new Aquarian Age place everything under the guidance of his sixth sense. Even the healing of the sick will be based on spirituality. This will no longer be an attempt to minimize the results of error and foolishness, but will take account of the soul as well as of the body; and through the healing of the aura, which shows the state of the etheric body, the physical body will be healed. Man's more highly developed intuition, and in many cases his newly found divine 'mind in the heart', will reveal to him those laws of healthy living which must be observed if he is to live on earth in the way that God intended.

A Star Brother does not seek solely to contact those beyond the grave but to commune with all the teachers and illumined ones of the land of Light. Even now all these illumined souls are drawing closer to help us clear away the mists of materialism — the Sages, the White Brethren, call them what you will — and folly so that we shall be able to live harmoniously with one another. We should establish peace and true brotherhood not just with those we find congenial — that is easy — but in a world-wide harmony that will better living conditions. We are told we should order our lives so that we help, not hinder the progress of our brother man. (I hope I am not repeating myself too often but relying, as I must, on the references to the New Age found in White Eagle literature; in trying to group what I find there within a single chapter, it is difficult not to be repetitive.) One of the most important factors in our spiritual evolution is the development of our power to project thought. How is thought used in the inner groups of the brotherhood? The brethren, duly prepared, meet in groups — much as brethren met in ancient times — to work with thought power which is cleansed of selfish motive and animated by the Christ love which is in the heart of the true brother. The brotherhood send forth thought power, concentrated and directed so that it will impinge on human receiving stations, the mind of man being receptive to thoughts of all kinds. The Masters, too, use concentrated thought power to purify and inspire humanity.

The Five Great Laws
These are the same as the cosmic laws which compromise the principles of the White Eagle Lodge, the first being reincarnation. We are well aware that not everyone accepts this truth, while an increasing number recognize it as a law of justice.

Reincarnation should certainly not be thought of as a continual and aimless transition between the earth and spirit realms. Each time the soul reincarnates it has a fresh opportunity to grow in cosmic consciousness. As it grows, its light — its soul light — grows stronger. The object of life is for the true Light of God to manifest through and illumine the darkness of densest matter. Reincarnation entails the periodic descent of each soul to labour in the world. In retrospect, each life seems only a flash, and the surviving soul returns to its true self in order to assimilate the lessons it has learnt.

In case this should sound rather terrifying, I would like to say that my companion, Ronald, managed to tell me very shortly after he passed that his guide is a grand personality and one full of laughter who teases him as they go through layer after layer of misdeeds and misconceptions: 'It's all so practical and sensible. I love every minute of my new life. Sometime I feel very humble and sad, but laughter predominates. We have the power to take the long view now and understand how every act worked for or against our development.' Why are we unable to remember our past lives? Quite a few people can. But the memory is in the higher or soul self, and until you are able to make contact with that you have only the memory relevant to your present existence.

Hypnotists have carried out experiments which leave little doubt that beneath normal consciousness lie hidden memories of lives and deaths from the frequently distant past. It is, however, most unwise to delve into past lives merely to satisfy one's curiosity. White Eagle was most firm about this, saying that memories of past lives will be awakened naturally at the right time and should not be forced. We can be very thankful that we are unable to remember past lives, for it can be very unwise to delve into these matters. White Eagle once said that many people think that karma is reaped only after death, but in fact some karma is almost immediate: if we eat too much, we are sick; if we are unkind to someone, they like us less. The memory of a past life seems to arrive when we are ready for it. We may have a psychically or spiritually advanced friend who will suddenly come out with information. After a series of meditations I was told by one member of the group that I had once been burnt to death and by another than I had had a violent death on a battlefield. I do not remember worrying much about either of these unsought revelations. Instant friendships and love have been by far the most comforting manifestations of karmic links, in my own experience.

The law of cause and effect is spoken of in the New Testament: 'Whatsoever a man soweth that shall he also reap.' We become accustomed to the sort of testings that give us the opportunity to learn whatever is our main lesson. Some of us seem to experience all our difficulties in our emotional life, while others learn more through their mental capacities. The fiery types, for example, have to learn the real meaning of love, which is the sun in man, whereas the earthy types are the practical folk who need to see the fruits of the earth, the results of what they do (see Appendix II). We must learn to think of life as a journey up the mountain of endeavour which leads to the peak where we can become aware. Once we achieve this awareness we become immune to sorrow and separation. It is really a question of acceptance. We may say glibly, 'Give us this day our daily bread', but too often when it arrives we grumble that there is no 'jam' on it!

The law of correspondences, or law of harmony, is that of the reflection between earth and heaven: 'As above, so below'. This means that the more we can reach up to the heavenly life, the more we can reflect it in our everyday earthly lives. But how, you may ask, should we not be sad when we have lost a beloved companion, or a child? Of course we miss those we have loved, but once we know the truth about death, and that it is truly a release from the selfness that is a death in life into the joy of selflessness in pure being, should we not instead control our very natural tears and rejoice for the one who has gone on? But more of this in the section on death (page 37).

Reincarnation will never separate you from your truly loved ones: this is impossible. In fact, we all have ages-old companions, some of whom we may have forgotten until they greet us again. While we should not grieve for the one who has left us, it is reasonable to grieve, though not excessively, for ourselves. I hope I have not given the impression that the reincarnation of one individual goes on through all eternity. Just as memory is something to do with the soul, so is rebirth. In all one's early stages, the soul outlives the body, but presumably when one has learnt all one can on earth, one will have outgrown the necessity to reincarnate. Eternal progress is of the spirit, the flame or sun-self.

Jesus The Christ

The Lodge teaches that the story of the birth of Jesus Christ at

Christmas is timeless and portrays a cosmic mystery in symbolic form. In all religions can be found the basic truth of the birth of the child, the Son of the Creator. It is asked even more frequently at the present time whether the story is true or merely symbolic. White Eagle says yes, it is a true story in itself, but it is also symbolic because it expresses a truth which has been repeated throughout the ages in the births of many Sun-Men who have appeared on earth at certain periods in order to unveil to humanity a little more of divine law and truth.

In ancient times men actually — and surprisingly — worshipped the sun and not just because it was the life-giver. They saw beyond it a spiritual power or influence that directed their lives; behind the physical sun they saw in the heavens was the spiritual radiation or life force on which their own lives depended. Life in every form is created through and sustained by the sun. As the heart is the life-giver and the power which motivates the physical body, so the sun is the heart of the solar system. Just as an aura surrounds the physical body, so from the sun there emanates a radiance, a spiritual illumination; and what is felt on earth in the form of heat and light is but a reflection of this radiance. 'In the beginning was the Word and the Word was with God and the Word was God.' 'God said, let there be light.' Light, then, was the first creation, the first created thing of God — the first-born, the Son of God. Therefore the words 'Christ, the first-born, the only begotten Son' refer to the Light created from the Being of God, that spiritual counterpart of the sun which is referred to as the Cosmic Christ. In the beginning, that aspect of God which is the Solar Logos drew together formless atoms and created form under the command of the Creator. This is the mystical meaning of the Immaculate Conception. The Son took form when He entered into virgin matter, and He created life on planet earth. This is the mystical truth underlying the story of the birth of the Child, the birth of the Christ. White Eagle says:

> The Cosmic Christ is not only a radiation, a power unseen and too often unfelt, the Cosmic Christ takes human form. We do not say that the whole radiation of the spiritual emanation from the Sun can, as it were, be crammed into one human form. We say that it can manifest in Great power through a perfect and beautiful human being.
>
> Children of earth pray to God, and sometimes God seems very

near, but when the human mind tries to think of the magnificence and glory of God the Father in terms of form, it entirely fails to comprehend. God caused the divine Son-Light to take human shape. It is the Light — or Son — in human form which creates a bridge between man and his Creator.

Many identify the person of Jesus of Nazareth with the bearer of the Christ Light. Let us get this clear. This Light is the first-born of the Father. Christ is of the Sun, the bearer of the Light. This glorious, radiant Being of Light whose aura permeates more than the earth, who is the light in all being in this planet, must surpass all human comprehension. It is not possible for this bearer of the Christ Light to descend and be born as an ordinary human being. He has no vehicle to draw Him down into incarnation on this earth. Therefore a vehicle was prepared for this purpose through many incarnations spent not only on earth but beginning even before humanity — as you understand it. Through many ages people have known that a great Being would some day descend from the Sun to save humanity from the depths of sin and error. This can be traced through many religions. At last came Jesus, the Master, the greatest soul ever incarnated in an earthly body, a Master who has prepared his spiritual bodies of vehicles to receive the tremendous inpouring of the great Sun-spirit, the Christ. Jesus, the Master was not of this earth's life stream. We mean by this that he was much older than this earth. He had been through experiences of a very exalted nature in preparation for his mission, the full power and implication of which is yet to be realized by earth people. The Master Jesus was a pure soul who had unfolded the inner glory. He came down from highest heaven to this earth planet step by step and took upon himself various bodies. All his incarnations were leading up to the appointed time when he would take the great incarnation which would radiate light and blessing. The spirit of Christ manifested through Jesus in a greater degree than it had ever manifested through another Master or teacher. This was the culmination of the Christ power which was and is to flood the earth and all mankind.

Jesus of Nazareth was trained in the Brotherhood of the Essenes, who taught the unfoldment of the inner light, who served the community in simple ways, tilling the soil, weaving, doing carpentry and all manner of handicraft. They were brethren with great love and gentleness in their hearts and lives. It was from this community the Master Jesus came — prepared both spiritually and physically to be the physical vehicle through which the glory of Christ would shine. Man will want to know whether others like Jesus will be born to manifest the Christ Light, or will it be a universal expression? As far as we can see it will be universal. That was the purpose of the coming of Christ through Jesus. There will come men who will be 'peaks of the human race', who will radiate the Christ light to a greater degree than lesser brethren. Even now there are some 'elder' brethren who radiate the Christ light in their degree, but their mission can never be the same as that of Jesus Christ, who gave himself for universal baptism and redemption — not in the old-fashioned sense as a physical atonement, but as an uprising and salvation for mankind.

'Salvation' is the right and only word to describe the mission of the Christ Spirit, for when the Christ Spirit comes alive in man he is literally saved from his sins. Thereafter man has nothing in the things of this world, once the Christ Spirit quickens within him and he has grown to full stature. This is the meaning of salvation for all humanity — not salvation through man's belief in one particular man, but salvation by reason of the Christ love within man himself. The Christ Light, the Son or the great Sun Spirit (the reflection of which you see manifested) would 'save' humanity by calling it into It's own substance and being, not to absorb the soul so that man loses his individuality, but rather to enlarge and expand his consciousness, so that in time he becomes at one with the Light. The mystery we are endeavouring to teach is this . . . that man is glorified by the Christ Spirit, and the purpose of man's life is that he shall glorify the flesh and glorify the earth, quicken the vibrations of physical matter and earthly matter until the whole planet becomes etherealized and spiritualized and returns once again into the bosom of the Father-Mother-God.

Christ the Son illuminates you, and releases you from the bondage of the world. Christ is more than the God-consciousness within. Christ is the radiance, the Light of the Sun, Christ is the power of the Sun, Christ is of the Father. 'The Father and I are one!' For from the heart of God was born the Son-the Light.

White Eagle ended this talk to students with the words:

We would like you to conceive this perfect human form of the Cosmic Christ as the saviour of earth's humanity. In your vision behold Him enthroned in unlimited space in the heavens. Not alone but surrounded by his younger brethren, all of who are creations of the Father-Mother-God, all part of His spirit, all part of the spirit of the whole — all brethren of the same spirit. You too — as at times you feel when you are in harmony and at one — are truly brethren, all of the same spirit. It is for you to seek this Divine Presence, to become attuned to it, to become at one with it. Our wish is that by these words you may understand that the Spiritual Son does manifest through a human form — the Cosmic Christ, whose life is being shed or radiated for earth's humanity. We have tried to open for you a consciousness, a realization, and a visualization that may help you, of this beloved and tender form of perfect humanity, through whom pours the splendour of the Spiritual Light upon you, loving, knowing and uplifting you always.

Death and the Hereafter

Death is the one thing that happens to all of us. You need no fortune-teller to tell you this, although some people are anxious, for one reason or another, to know the approximate year when it will come to them. But for those — and they are many — who accept the truth of reincarnation, death ceases to be alarming, for it can be seen as a recurring event in a long life cycle. It is untrue to say that there is no literature on this subject. The White Eagle Lodge publishes many books on survival, reincarnation and kindred subjects. The College of Psychic Studies is only too happy to lend books from its library or help individuals to contact the sort of medium most suited to their particular need: for example, if a person's interests are chiefly material it is better for him not to consult one who operates at a high spiritual level.

From the very beginning of his ministry, White Eagle discouraged the presence of any sort of physical phenomena at his Lodge. Indeed, he said that to dabble in such phenomena without knowledge of the laws that govern them is as dangerous as for a child to play with electrical installations. It seems that spiritualistic phenomena were produced for a limited period in order to shake man out of his materialism and awaken him to occult truths. Now the need for this is passing, and those who are to some extent awakened should be ready for the next and more difficult step, which is not one to be taken lightly. This is to become aware of the inner or higher worlds, and it can only be achieved through prayer and self-discipline. Yet it is a fact that everyone can enlarge the scope of his consciousness and communicate not only with friends and relations who have died but also with guides and teachers who will help them with their work and service on earth.

As to where we all go, the astral world where we awaken after death may be described as an inner or finer world. It is not a world as the hymn says 'above the bright blue sky' but one that interpenetrates the physical world yet remains invisible because it vibrates faster. Thus souls after death awaken to a different state of consciousness rather than to a different place. Indeed, many people who die suddenly or unexpectedly have no idea that they are dead, and it can take some quite a while to understand what has happened to them. Often enough it is a very ordinary thing that impresses them. In Cynthia, the Lady Sandy's book *The Awakening Letters*, this clairaudient writer records how her own dead brother told her that he had wanted to get out of bed and had asked for his clothes and shaving kit, only to be told, 'All that *just happens* here'. [8] Several other people who on 'awakening' communicated with Cynthia had been surprised to discover the same thing.

It would seem from the other side that the fear of death is man's greatest bogey. For this reason, when a person is able to free himself of this and truly rejoice when a loved one is freed from a restrictive old body, he has made a great step forward. Life in the inner world is not only a world of thought but also one of feeling. Thought is at the next level to the physical, but as you penetrate behind thought you come to the world of feeling and emotion. The recognition and control of our own bodies of feeling and emotion is one of the first lessons to be learnt if we want to develop spiritual insight; uncontrolled feelings lead to storms. When we die, our soul passes through the lower planes until we reach the one where we belong, and this will then seem as solid as the world now seems to us. The rise to a heavenly world is not immediate: different stages have to be passed through, rather as we endure various tests in the course of our earthly lives.

White Eagle taught that the first thing a man awakens to after death is *a world of his own creation:* 'Heaven is what you make it'. Like attracts like, so if he has been selfish he will find selfish spirit people around him; his environment will be a replica of his inner self, himself externalized. And whatever is ugly is intensified, because over there one cannot disguise or conceal the truth. It is hard to describe the wonder and, above all, the freedom of the spirit world. People there have only to think or wish to be in a particular place and they are there: if, for example, they create in their minds a beautiful garden with flowers and shrubs, they are actually in that garden. In short, their thoughts or dreams become their realities.

3. The Work

Discovering the Lodge

If you have never been to a particular place, you wonder what goes on there. As far as the White Eagle Lodge is concerned, if you are in need of healing, you may come first to one of the contact healing services or to the Sunday service. These are held both at the country headquarters in Liss, Hampshire and in Kensington, London; also at daughter lodges and groups in the UK and elsewhere. It is as well to arrive in good time for your treatment to be arranged. You will not be required to undress, though shoes or boots should be taken off. The time will then come for you to be called by the chief healer to take your place on one of the stools where those to receive healing sit.

On entering the temple or place where healing is given you may be conscious of a loving, welcoming feeling. This feeling of belonging is often remarked on: 'I felt I'd come home,' I have heard said many times. And indeed, if you *do* belong, this is a wonderful feeling. Sometimes, when showing people over the place, I have nearly been knocked over: the strength of the greeting can be very strong indeed. I feel it to be an angelic greeting. Those familiar with Mendelssohn's fairy music will recall the twittering, trembling vibrations of his *A Midsummer Night's Dream*. The sound I am referring to seems to be the same type of vibration but on a larger scale, so I feel it must be emitted by angels. Every human being has a guardian angel — this is no fairy tale — so surely it is natural that someone's own angel is pleased to have an opportunity to make its presence felt? I only wish I could see angels, but being a fairly down-to-earth sort of person I find that my way of registering other-worldly contacts is for the most part through physical sensation. Many people 'see' while meditating; I only 'know'. It may be just a case of a brief *frisson* or a sensation like that described above.

White Eagle told us that to find inner truth one thing is essential: purity of life. By this he did not mean asceticism. The aspirant today is not concerned with a monastic or ascetic life but is called upon to mix with humanity and to carry Light into the world, bringing it to everyone he encounters. Most people who discover the Lodge's work do so through reading one of the books. When they write to obtain further teaching, they are informed whether there is a lodge or group near them; if they so wish they can become a part of the work of that group.

Collective Worship
Collective worship or, ordinarily speaking, 'going to church' does not appeal to everyone. One friend of mine simply cannot stand hymn singing, while another comes to services because she so enjoys singing hymns. You cannot please everybody. Yet it is not possible for some of us to seek peace in our own inmost sanctuary, and even a daily quiet time can be subject to constant interruption. Communal worship is thus valuable. It can help us to break through the thought-forms immediately surrounding the world.

Jesus said: 'Where two or three are gathered together in my name, there am I in the midst of them.' Joan Hodgson has said much that is helpful on this subject.[1] She reminds us that what happens in collective worship is that strong, aspiring thought-forms are created. These cut through the lower astral and mental spheres like a shaft of light. Like Jacob's ladder, this light reaches the higher worlds. Down the ladder come shining ones, angels and ministers of grace and even our own beloved friends who have left this life — changed their address, we might say. In this way those who are stronger help those who are less successful on their own: unity of aspiration gives increased strength, the combined power of a group being greater than that of any member working alone.

The key of the door to the inner world lies on our side of it, and until we turn that key even our own beloved who is longing to help us cannot come through the door. When you see a White Eagle Lodge service mentioned in a calendar, it is described as we shall be able to direct that golden radiance to any afflicted part. That same radiance will eventually transform the corruptible body into an incorruptible one.

Jesus taught that the suffering of others is our concern. Every soul who aspires with humility to serve can be trained to be a healer and comforter of humanity. Of course, there are many methods and combinations of methods, and the healer should satisfy himself that necessary medical advice and treatment has first been sought. I personally have undergone several operations while simultaneously being helped by a healing group. I well remember the staff nurse asking me how I felt on emerging from the anaesthetic. 'Fine,' was my reply. 'Liar!' was her reaction. But it was true; I did feel fine, and had no sickness or headache and best of all, no sense of anxiety. Pain, too, was kept to a minimum.

The mixing of different methods of spiritual healing is not recommended. This is rather like listening to two music programmes at the same time: neither can be appreciated. The method of healing practised at the White Eagle Lodge involves co-operation with the angels of healing in order to direct the prescribed colour ray to the chakra concerned. The following colours are used in varying depths: red, gold, green, blue, amethyst, violet, and finally, the pearl or Christ Light. One should try to see these colours as though they were shining through a stained glass window and entering the chakra as a healing beam. Healing works gently on the condition and considering the number of years this condition may have taken to build up in the soul-body, a corresponding length of time may have to pass before any improvement shows in the physical body. What can arrive without delay, however, are a sense of peace and an increased ability to cope with life. The colour ray healing given at the Lodge is either contact healing, which takes place at a healing service, or what is known as absent healing, in which the rays can be sent any distance. Patients are told how to co-operate, and the power of the healing depends on the strength of the magical link of the group's leader with the Star Brotherhood. Those healers who are members of the White Eagle Lodge and other individuals who want wholeheartedly to become part of this spiritual work can apply to join the White Eagle Brotherhood.

Sex, Karma and Healing
There is no doubt that sexual union touches the deepest springs

of man's being and so is a potent means of creating or working out karma. Why should some couples try for years with no success to have children, while in other families determined babies seem to evade the 'safest' methods of birth control? At the present time, women are being helped to have babies by what is rather stupidly termed the 'test-tube' method. Except for the fact that it is not always their husband's child, it seems a perfectly legitimate and very kindly medical intervention. What is unkind is for the child to be called a 'test-tube baby', which could lead to it being teased at school.

Then there is the question of abortion. Undertaken with proper medical care, this is infinitely preferable to the backroom experiments of the past. Yet instinctively, women feel that abortion is wrong; they long to protect and love the little life within them. I personally have known cases where, pressurized by so-called friends, a girl has undergone an abortion. The scar left in her soul-memory shows in her face in the form of an enduring sadness: without realizing it, she knows that life is a precious gift from God. Yet everything depends on the motive behind this sad decision: if that motive is not wholly selfish, it may still bring sadness, but loving, caring action is always blessed. It is possible that heavy karma for incarnations ahead results only from selfish action taken for the sake either of convenience or of sensual gratification.

What does White Eagle say about sex? He agrees with most spiritual teachers that it should be enjoyed only within a dedicated partnership wherein each partner takes full responsibility for the happiness and well-being of the other. Responsibility is the keynote: there is no place for promiscuity. He is not of the opinion that divorce is necessarily wrong. The time may have arrived when both partners have discharged some debt of long standing and so freed themselves from something that each had hitherto felt the need to cope with, in which case there need be no bitterness. This is entirely a matter for the individual conscience. It may happen that one partner exerts excessive power in the form of a magnetic emotional tie which causes the other to become completely dominated. Here it may be hard for the one who suffers to make the break, but divorce is clearly the best answer, and great courage is needed in order to face the inevitable loneliness.

Responsible, kind fatherhood, loving, wise motherhood, a happy, united family life — these have been the ideals of great races and civilizations throughout the ages. For a woman, sexual union normally awakens deep feelings which are a preparation for the natural completion of the act in motherhood; this is why sex outside marriage can be psychologically damaging, quite apart from the risk of unwanted children. On the whole it is no longer considered wrong for men and women to live together without marrying. This does not alter the fact that as soon as they live together a mystical and karmic bond is created. Whether or not they have children, they have taken upon themselves the responsibilities of marriage and all it entails. Because marriage is so deeply karmic it surely seems right to set forth on this path with a religious ceremony invoking God's help and blessing. These days society looks more kindly than formerly on the single mother, but the father must not suppose that he goes scot-free. In a future life, and perhaps in a woman's body, he will go through an almost identical experience; not only that but he may actually be born as the unwanted child of a similar union.

These are not the only problems that man feels guilty about. Homosexuality has always existed, though it was hidden and suppressed in the sex-fearing Victorian era. In recent years many young people have even been afraid to enjoy friendship with those of their own sex. If their early emotional life blossoms in this way they may feel quite unnecessarily tormented, whereas in fact this can be a perfectly normal awakening in preparation for a deeper and more satisfying partnership with a member of the opposite sex. What is the underlying cause of homosexuality? After a number of lives, say in a man's body, it may be hard for a particular soul to adjust to the new dimension of a woman's body, and it will continue to feel emotionally attracted to other women; the reverse is also the case. A further cause of homosexuality may be that the soul in question has spent an incarnation in a monastery or a convent. He or she may then prefer the companionship in this life of the sex he or she became accustomed to in a previous life. Everything depends on a soul's past experience.

Last but by no means least, as far as shame and the sense of guilt is concerned, is incest. The need for secrecy here is stronger than in any other perversion, for more than one member of a family is involved. The twentieth century has brought freedom of speech on almost every formerly forbidden subject, but we have yet to see a play on this subject, at least to my knowledge. I myself have come across it in my capacity as psychological astrologer, and I reacted to it exactly as I do to any complex relationship. In this case I had to deal with the younger generation. What helped the girl in question most was that we were able to discuss a comparison with her own of her father's astrological chart, which threw light on the whole situation and gave me the opportunity to make an educated guess as to the karmic causes.

Animals and Healing

Animals respond very sensitively to healing and are good proof that such spiritual healing is not merely psychological. The Lodge's animal healing is organized by the East Sussex Daughter Lodge.

Many people who have sick pets long to heal them but do not know how to go about this. They fail to realize that they could be splendid healers if they focused their aspirations on God, the Great White Spirit. True healing power, for humans and animals, is love: human love illumined by the divine Love which can flow through your hands as light, the healing Light which restores first the etheric and then the physical body. I now quote Joan Hodgson on the subject:

> If you desire to heal your own pet, choose a time when the animal is quietly settled in a comfortable position and sit beside it so that you can easily stroke its spine gently from head to tail. Try to put aside all worry and anxiety and focus your whole being on the great light and love of God. It is easiest to visualize this great light as the Sun, the spiritual power behind and within the Sun. Try to imagine this great light pouring into your head and heart and flowing through your right hand as you gently but firmly stroke your pet's spine, starting from the brow, over the head and right along the spine. Just see the stream of light flowing into your pet as you keep on quietly stroking and firmly holding the thought of God.
>
> It is not so much the stroking as the focusing your whole being on God that is important. The more clearly you can hold the concentration, the more the healing power will flow through you. With practice you will be able to hold it clearly for several minutes and may become conscious of a great warmth, almost a tingling sensation in your right hand, as if an electric current were pouring through you. Do not force yourself to hold it for too long. Go on gently and peacefully for a minute or two, then stop. Mentally ask for the blessing of the Great White Spirit and pray that the angels of healing will continue the work. Be sure to wash your hands thoroughly after giving this treatment and be at peace,

knowing your pet is in good hands. Animals are remarkably responsive to spiritual healing: far more so than humans, because they do not put up any mental resistance. If your animal has not 'heard the call', he or she will surely respond to the healing. If however its time has come to withdraw into the inner world, try to realize that for an animal the world of spirit, or the etheric world, is not far removed from the life it knows. Animals who are loved do not go far away but live in the spirit home of their master or mistress and are with them during their hours of sleep. The spirit world closely penetrates the physical world almost as water penetrates a sponge. Your animal who dies is hardly aware of any difference, except that life is much more fun and it feels better.

I remember watching with some heartbreak the passing of a beloved bitch. It was a beautiful experience. As she breathed her last I suddenly became aware of a dear relative in the spirit world standing near and he gave a little whistle. As he did so I saw Mandy rise up out of her dead body and stretch herself just as she did when waking from sleep. Then she gave a little shake and went towards him, wagging her tail, full of life and joy just as if she were setting off on a lovely country walk. For a long time after this we were aware of her often in her old haunts in the house and know she was not really conscious of any difference. I firmly believe that the love which humans bear to animals helps them in their evolution and that quite often they reincarnate and come back to the same master or mistress at the appointed time.[6]

I have reproduced the whole of the article in question, as Joan is more sensitive than I am; whereas I too have had the experience of pets dying, I cannot tell you so vividly of the inner experience. But it is a fact that I have never lost a pet without making some contact with it afterwards. A Scottie dog of mine was run over while I was away from it. I dreamt that my mother phoned me with the news, which lessened the shock of hearing it on my return. After the death of my next Scottie, the animal came from a higher level to give me a rapturous greeting; this, too, was in a dream.

Those who work for or make contributions to animal welfare under the 'endangered species' heading will be glad to know that these are not forgotten in Lodge prayers for animals; neither are the many creatures who suffer through man's greed and cruelty.

The Star Brotherhood
The Star Brotherhood is what was formerly known as the White Brotherhood. This term was dropped because it could have been

interpreted to mean that there were no black brothers, which is very far from the truth. White Eagle reminded us that we are all at different stages of the evolutionary ladder. Many are toiling in darkness; some have their faces raised towards the sun. Some have climbed only a little way up the mountain side, while others are higher on it. On the peaks are the shining ones who look with love and compassion on humanity. Souls who have expanded in consciousness and become truly aware of goodness and beauty, knowledge and wisdom look at earthly things from a viewpoint that is very different from that of men and women at the lower levels. With a heightened awareness of God, man sees with a truer perspective and benefits more directly from the rays of love or light which come down from the great ones. These beings have as their object the helping forward of man's spiritual evolution. This ancient brotherhood has always been in existence, even though at times it has been driven into secret places in remote parts of the earth. Never has God left man without a witness to Himself.

Records of such brotherhoods exist in the Himalayas, in what White Eagle referred to as the holy centre of the Middle East, in the Andes and in the far north and in Britain. Though records of these great fraternities have in places been graven in stone, more often the memory lies deep within the souls of men who were admitted to an inner brotherhood in some distant incarnation. It is wisest to think of the ancient brotherhood as a universal body composed of the great teachers and saints of all ages, not excluding many of their disciples. However, other beings exist which are superior to even the greatest of these. All — and White Eagle reminded us that when he said 'all', he included the planetary and angelic beings who work with humanity on earth — all come under the direction of the one supreme Lord or Christ, the supreme Light of all. Who are these great ones? They are human souls who, through a succession of lives, have learnt how to unfold their God-nature. Some received their teaching from God-Men, who came from other and more highly evolved planets to establish knowledge of God on earth and teach early man how to use his own inner powers. It is necessary to know that such ones, who are masters of matter and of all earthly things, always conceal their greatness: an ancient brother will never disclose his secret. The greater the brother, the more ordinary he will seem, mingling with his fellows, entering into their interests, joys and sorrows and doing what he can to comfort them and to illumine the road along which they are travelling.

Masters and elder brethren exist, unknown to mankind in general, all over the world. These make no claims, but work silently behind the scenes of human life to influence men and their leaders. They give their help to certain groups and religious organizations. Indeed, all groups born with the ideal of service and brotherhood have behind them one or more of the elder brethren who lend power and guidance to that group. The masters of the Star Brotherhood are universal in their service; they are behind all institutions working for mankind. Their centres or lodges exist all over the earth in places unknown to the outside world. The outside world is not allowed to intrude on these sanctuaries of the brotherhood where the elder brethren meet and from which they direct power and Light to mankind. Masters really do exist. They either inhabit a physical body and move about amongst mankind or dwell in quiet and remote places. If their work requires it, they will appear in cities. They are on the alert to help, to link up with those ready to receive their teaching or to be used in the service to the brotherhood. They can perform what we call miracles, because they have learnt to free themselves from the bondage of flesh. They are true yogis who possess the secret of union of the lower or physical self with the divine.

The power to be unhampered by the limitations of the flesh is within the capacity of each one of us; it is not limited to a few elect souls. The Masters only use power for a special purpose and for the good of mankind, never for vulgar display or to demonstrate how clever they are. An elder brother might walk into your lodge, and, unless you noticed the light on his face or perceived the gentleness and sweetness of his entire nature, you would not realize he was a Master. He would not make any spectacular demonstration. One might ask: 'Can we, who are only of the mass of humanity, in any way be linked to this brotherhood of the Masters?' You do not need to pass through any particular school in order to become their pupil. No earthly form or ceremony of initiation will of itself link you with the Star Brotherhood. Race, caste and creed make no difference. Brotherhood is contained in the heart: a soul quite ignorant of occult teaching may yet be an initiate. Many souls who qualify for initiation have done so unconsciously; the purity of their lives, aspirations and motives draws them towards the Great White

Light as naturally as steel is drawn to a magnet. The core of all brotherhood, whether of today or of millions of years ago, is the inner Light.

In Britain we had the Rosicrucians, and many people today are interested in their teachings. White Eagle states that the Brotherhood of the Rose-Cross has existed since ancient times, but we are now speaking of that Rosicrucian brotherhood which was one of the early mystery schools, whereby certain ideals were reintroduced to men and women sufficiently advanced to be able to understand and put them into practice. This group was established by a few initiates in the sixteenth century, a crucial period in the history of the Western world. Francis Bacon and the Comte de St Germain are two names associated with it. Mystery still surrounds these men, as it does the alchemists of the Middle Ages, but those who have studied the matter agree that these brethren released a wonderful light for the illumination of mankind and did a great deal for the advancement of learning. It was at that time that the true spiritual light in man for this New Age began to reveal itself. White Eagle wanted it to be clear that the majority of the Rosicrucian brethren are in the invisible realms. You cannot become a Rosicrucian merely by joining a society on earth; you become a Rosicrucian by the quality of your life and your quiet, simple ways.

The plain truth is that brotherhoods at their highest level share a common denominator which is in the measure of Christ Consciousness: Christ is the common denominator of all life. The Spirit of God or the divine in man manifests itself in human souls. The cross is the oldest known symbol, and it represents man as he stands, with feet together and head erect: his feet on earth, his head in the heavens and his arms stretched outwards in service and sacrifice. Yet when man begins to recognize the divinity in all men, his service to his brother is no longer a sacrifice but a joy. Surrounding, enfolding, the cross is the universal symbol of the sun: the circle. This circle of light and love which is the spiritual counterpart of the sun shines in the hearts of true brothers. It is a flame invisible to human eyes, just as there is within every man another, invisible man born not of flesh but of water and spirit — a sun-self. We should acknowledge the presence both in the sun and in ourselves of a transcendent Being. The complete symbol of the brotherhood is a star in the centre of a cross of light set within a circle of light. Through a continual linking with that six-pointed star the members of the White Eagle Lodge send out healing to the whole of humanity. This link is created through prayer and meditation, which are the means by which the Light is sent out into the world. This task is fundamental to the Lodge's work.

4. Links with Other Groups

Members and Friends

The White Eagle Lodge is an independent legal entity, registered as a charitable trust under the 1960 Charities Act. It is hardly surprising that relations with other organizations should always have been friendly, for White Eagle insists that such things as race, colour and creed should play no part in the Lodge. Embracing as it does much of the philosophy of the Eastern religions, the beauty of esoteric Christianity and the spiritualistic knowledge of the continuity of life after death, the White Eagle Lodge has an affinity with all the major religions in their original inspiration, if not with their subsequent dogmas. There are many Quakers among Lodge members, for there is a particular closeness between their own and the Lodge's way of thinking. A friendly link exists with the local Buddhist community and also with the Sri Chinmoy group.

Minesta (Grace Cooke) had a lifelong friendship with Maurice Barbanell and his wife Sylvia; both she and Ivan Cooke wrote regularly for *Psychic News*. This friendship dated from when Maurice, then a very young reporter, wrote of a meeting taken by Minesta. The College of Psychic Studies also has links with the Lodge. Two of its longest-serving presidents, Brigadier Roy Firebrace and Paul Beard, were or are also part of the Lodge's work.

Increasing harmony is evident with the various New Age groups, and there is a mutual interest and respect between the Lodge and Sir George Trevelyan's Wrekin Trust, Theo Gimbel's Hygeia Studios and Peter Dawkins's Gatekeepers' Trust. The late

Clare Cameron, for so many years editor of the *Science of Thought Review*, a monthly magazine devoted to the teaching of applied right thinking and founded by Henry Thomas Hamblin, will be missed at the Lodge, where she regularly attended Sunday services. Links are growing with the main yoga groups, and the names Howard Kent and Ickwellbury spring to mind, as does the Iyengar Foundation in India, where the Lodge's yoga leader was taught. A strong sympathy exists with Compassion in World Farming and Beauty Without Cruelty, both of which were founded through the inspiration of White Eagle and the Cookes. As for America, Jean Le Fevre, formerly leader of the Crowborough Daughter Lodge, is now based there and is the representative of the Lodge near Houston, Texas. She has established a close link with the Seneca Indians and is establishing another with Unity.

Who are the members? It is fair to say that they are a very varied cross-section of mankind. Interest in the White Eagle Lodge's work has grown steadily without any violent ups and downs. World membership, now around 4,000, increases by three to four hundred members a year. Media exposure has been remarkably small. In 1974 BBC South televised a thirty-minute programme about the opening of the Temple at Rake. This attracted favourable press comments and local comment. However, publicity about the Lodge has been limited to articles in the specialist press, including *Psychic News, The Vegetarian* and similar papers. It is largely through reading the books that people join the Lodge. The White Eagle books are stocked widely. The Greater World Association, the Spiritualist Association of Great Britain, and the S.N.U. at Stansted Hall all keep them, as does the *Psychic News* bookshop and mail order organization.

This brings me to the work of the White Eagle Publishing Trust.

The White Eagle Publishing Trust
It was the publication in 1932 of the first book about the teaching of White Eagle *Thy Kingdom Come* that led to the establishing of the White Eagle Lodge four years later. The Lodge's publishing activities have continued since then, initial print orders being for 1,000 books at a time; growth of sales has been steady, however, and nowadays they are for anything from 6,000 to 12,000. In 1953, under White Eagle's guidance, the White Eagle Publishing Trust was formed. During the 1970s sales increased dramatically,

and in recent years some 50,000 have been sold each year of the religious books, that is to say, excluding the books on vegetarianism. As not all members possess copies of all the books, it can be seen that the vast majority of books are sold to other interested enquirers. This is especially true of the little book *The Quiet Mind* which will soon have sold its hundred thousandth copy.[1]

Appendix A:
White Eagle Teaching and Yoga

White Eagle reminds us that there are yogis in the Western as well as in the Eastern world, but says that we will not know them, for they do not proclaim themselves, preferring to work quietly in the background. They are all directing this same power, this Light, out into the world. If this were not so, the world would be impossible to live in. Thus we are reminded that the role of the yogi is that of a channel through which the Light may flow into the darkness of matter. This, too, is the essence of White Eagle's teaching: that we should become ever purer channels through which the Christ Light can manifest itself.

In yoga, we attempt to attain a subtle balance between the physical, mental and spiritual energies because such a state of harmony allows the divine Light to flow more freely. Where there is an absence of stress and tension both in the physical body and in the mind, where the emotions are under control and there is poise between all the elements of the self, then the channel is pure and the power is strong. White Eagle has often said that the body is the temple of the spirit: a view that is shared by many oriental yogis. It is therefore our duty to preserve and purify our 'temples' so that we are better able to serve humanity.

In the practice of yoga, we try to do just this. Through certain postures and the control of the breath the life force or *prana* is harnessed, co-ordinating the two energy streams, the physical and the mental, so that these work in harmony and not in opposition. We learn to relax the whole physical body and the mind, letting go of the unavoidable tensions and stresses of modern life. In this quiescent state the prepared vessel is ready to receive, through meditation, the nectar of the spirit, the radiating Light. Thus in our communion with the Christ Spirit, in our quiet moments, in our meditations or hours spent with healing groups, we make closer contact and become purer channels for the Master. This, then, is our purpose in practising yoga. At the same time we experience other benefits, namely a healthier body, a clearer mind and a more joyous disposition — all of which are true complements to the White Eagle way of life.

Considerable emphasis is placed on correct breathing and on the rhythm of the individual breath, with the recognition that each person has his own breathing pattern. The breath and the mind are directly linked, and by control and regulation of the breath we can quieten the mind, promoting tranquillity and a sense of inner peace. Likewise with the *asanas* or postures. When performed with the rhythm of the breath they transform the physical movement into a spiritual experience, bringing a stillness and an awareness of the truth that all life is one. We are told the value of Star breathing and breathing in the divine Light, and it is through this that one should approach the postures. Classes are held both at New Lands and at the London Lodge.

Appendix B:
White Eagle Astrology

If you want an esoteric angle on the subject, you can do no better than read Joan Hodgson. Her first book, *Wisdom in the Stars*, written in 1943, was published under her maiden name of Cooke, but this has been through various editions and reprints, the latest being in 1980, under her present surname. This book, together with the 1979 edition of *Why on Earth?* are highly recommended to those who want to know more about reincarnation.

One could say that astrology falls into two categories: Firstly, there is the exoteric kind, seen at a very superficial level in newspapers and magazines and chiefly concerned with light character analysis and rough predictions based only on the sun sign. It is impossible to work seriously on this meagre basis; what is needed is a knowledge of the whole balance of an individual's birth chart.

The esoteric approach to the subject, as taught in the White Eagle School of Astrology, is quite a different matter. It entails the study of the spiritual laws which guide the evolution of humanity, the heavenly principles which lie behind all material manifestation. Its basis is the universal law of correspondences recognized by the ancient wisdom and expressed simply in the words: 'As above (in the heavens) so below (on earth); as below, so above.' In order to understand astrology at its profound level the student needs to understand and accept this spiritual law, together with those of reincarnation, karma (cause and effect), opportunity (the idea that we are placed in conditions which provide exactly those opportunities which are necessary for our soul's growth and development) and balance or equilibrium (which causes the soul to pass through the opposing or balancing experiences of joy and sorrow, labour and rest, day and night — in effect, the constant ebb and flow of the tides of life). Truly esoteric astrology should be the study of the working out in human life of these great laws, which correspond to the planets and constellations. As Joan says: 'The gulf which is between this and the average exoteric astrology is as wide as the gulf which separates "pop" music from a Beethoven symphony.'

Man is part of nature. Plant, bird, beast and man are all dependent for their existence on the sun, the earth, the air and the rain, in short, upon the interaction of the four elements. Yet it does not occur to everyone that our souls are also fed and nurtured by the spiritual counterpart of each of the four elements. These elements have been from ancient times associated with the twelve signs of the zodiac. Each sign is said to 'belong' to a certain element, and each element finds threefold expression through the three signs allotted to it. This threefold expression is analagous to the triune aspects of God, the twelve signs falling into four groups of three. By their known relationship with certain signs, the planets are also intimately connected with the elements. During the Middle Ages the idea was universally held that man was a being composed of the various elements in varying proportions. As Mark Antony says of Brutus in the play *Julius Caesar*:

> His life was gentle, and the elements
> So mixed in him that Nature might stand up
> And say to all the world, 'This was a man!'

Materialists may scoff, but the fact remains that a competent astrologer, can, by studying the chart of the heavens drawn up for the moment and place of birth of a person, draw up a remarkably accurate picture of an individual's temperament.

In daily life, and with or without astrological knowledge, it is possible to see which of the elements predominates in the make-up of each of our associates. If it is fire, they are lovable, hasty, generous, and enthusiastic about any person or project appealing to their feelings; their hearts run away with their heads. In the olden days they would have been classed as having the 'choleric' or fiery temperament. When found to be suffering from feverish or inflammatory ills they would have been given soothing and cooling treatment. Others are recognizable as 'melancholic' or earthy types. These are placid, calm and collected, not given to excitement or enthusiasm. Practical and full of common sense — not given to flights of fancy — they are well suited to the handling of material problems. They need plenty of exercise, as they are prone to complaints caused by a clogging of the system. The airy or 'sanguine' types, on the other hand, are interested in reading and study, preferring theory to practice. Their taste and artistic talents will show in their homes in their feeling for colour and harmony. Any health problems they might have are often the result of overstrained nerves or mental stress, and they need to learn mental or thought control.

Finally come the 'phlegmatic' types, in whom the water element plays the strongest part. These people tend to carry the burdens of the world on their shoulders. Water people tend to imagine slights where none are intended; when this happens they can be moody or sulky. But though timid and retiring, they can also be courageous, enduring life's tests bravely. They are often physically receptive, although I personally have found that it is frequently the very communicative airy types who excel as mediums. When I gave a talk on this once, many of the water types present were incensed, and protested, 'No, we are the sensitives!' So they may be, but as I have said, one needs the full individual chart in order to make a true assessment. It is through the study of our starry pattern that we can learn to know ourselves.

Long ago the mysteries of the lessons to be learnt by the spirit became clothed in fairy tales and fables. The tests which every soul undergoes before it can master the elements are presented in fairy tales as seemingly impossible tasks which the hero must attempt; every soul is a hero embarked on an arduous test. The Bible, too, is full of such allegories, through which we can unfold heavenly secrets.

Just as the physical sun is sign and symbol of a greater spiritual Sun, God the Father, the Creator, so within man there dwells a spark of God that is like a tiny sun. This helps us to understand the biblical statement that God created man 'in His own image': The light of love which shines as a sun within the heart of every man is one with the Great Architect of the universe.

How does White Eagle astrology compare with that taught by other groups and associations? Joan Hodgson obtained her diploma from the Faculty of Astrological Studies before 1950 and has been a member of the Astrological Association of Great

Britain, for whom she has occasionally written articles. She considers herself a very basic astrologer and conventional in her approach, although there is no denying that her approach is from the esoteric angle. Although both Joan and I have great admiration for many of the writings of Alice Bailey, we feel that to have a deep understanding of her astrological writings would involve scrapping our own long years of basic study. I am therefore not prepared to comment further, except to state that Alice Bailey entitles one of her works *Esoteric Astrology*.[1] Yet much of it is so far from basic understanding of the subject as to be incomprehensible to the average student. The late Alan Leo, on the other hand, wrote both interestingly and comprehensibly on both basic and esoterically approached astrology. Many of his writings have been quoted in White Eagle astrology.

More recently there has been a book by A. G. S. Norris called *Transcendental Astrology*.[2] This book takes numerology into account and is in many ways closer to the White Eagle approach than to the intellectual or scientific angle taken in the Alice Bailey books. However, all these books will be of interest only to astrologers. Of the above, the White Eagle approach is the simplest, and it encourages the development of intuitive perception in its pupils. The 'feel' of the planets plays a big part, and a comprehensive study both of the rays and meditation is written of in Joan Hodgson's more recent books. Her chief interest is in the deeper, spiritual issues. 'Esoteric' means 'secret or mysterious' or, according to certain dictionaries, 'meaningful only to the initiated'. 'Transcendental' means 'transcending the ordinary range of perception or conception', so the two terms are really quite close.

Nobody really knows how long a knowledge of the interrelation between the constellations or signs of the zodiac and human life has been with mankind. Astrology has been part of man's understanding from prehistoric times. Inscriptions on stone monuments and the designs of temples such as Stonehenge point to the fact that long before recorded history man had knowledge of the movements of heavenly bodies. White Eagle teaches that this knowledge was brought to earth by God-Men whose task it was to care for and educate their infant humanity.

Astrology is so much more than a method of prediction or even of character reading: it touches the deepest springs of being. It is taught in the White Eagle Lodge, that is to say, a course is offered for those who seek in this subject a key to man's spiritual evolution. Regular meetings are held in London, and an annual conference at New Lands. Instruction is by correspondence course at three levels which are designed to guide the student from being a novice to becoming a professionally qualified astrologer. The courses culminate in a diploma examination. The middle or intermediate level suits those who already know how to calculate a chart, and six lessons take such students to a point where they may embark on the advanced course. All necessary material is supplied with the lessons, and each student receives individual tuition. Details may be obtained from the office at New Lands.

Appendix C:
The Lodge's Younger Members

You may think this information applies only to those who have children or grandchildren, but I am reliably informed that many older people say they have learnt a great deal from the so-called children's books and newsletters because these really start at the beginning and are something which they themselves missed out on when they were small. Happily, in the Lodge, children of any age are well catered for. Usually when Sunday services are held in the Temple there is also a service for children in the chapel at New Lands: Children can attend this while their parents enjoy the Temple service in peace. This is also the case in some daughter lodges and groups.

The White Eagle Lodge magazine, *Stella Polaris*, has articles for young readers and also, occasionally, sections for children and parents. These are a great help to those living far away or those who run groups where there are children wanting to take part in the Lodge activities.

Everyone who joins the children's group is sent a badge of a six-pointed star to wear and told it will remind him or her of the light in the heart which can shine like a star, filling the world with Light and Love. The motto given to all who apply for this badge is 'I serve (God and His family)'. White Eagle would like them all — every brother and member of the Lodge — to hold these words in their hearts and let them be their guide throughout their lives.

The books of spiritual teaching for children now available are proving helpful to those of all denominations. Jenny Dent, who wrote the more recent children's books, finds that many children take naturally to meditation, but they all need patient help from parents. At whatever age you start meditation, regular practice is essential, firstly to train the physical body and mind to keep still. This will assist concentration. As you gradually close the physical senses to the outer world during your period of meditation you become more aware of the still centre deep within your heart. This is the true purpose of meditation, for it entails seeking to become at one with God's light within your own heart as well as with His great Light which shines within all creation. Having made this contact with God we hope to become gradually illumined with His Light and qualities so that we can be of better service. Our 'outgiving' in service is essential, for our motive should not be spiritual progress for ourselves but the desire to be better channels through which God's light can shine out into the world. It is a good idea to establish a meditation and prayer time in a child's routine from a very early age. You may have to have different times for different age groups, as little ones may disturb the older children who are ready for a longer period of silence. Try to create a happy family time when they know that they have your full love and attention; in this way they will look forward to it.

As for the position, a simple cross-legged posture or kneeling with feet tucked under is best. (A special rug or their own yoga mat is a help.) The child must feel comfortable and relaxed. Hands should be clasped loosely in the lap, the left hand cupped in the right, or both held together in the traditional posture for prayer. Jenny tells children to think of their hands like this as forming the symbol of the little flame of God that burns in their hearts. To begin with, keep the silent concentration for only a few moments, gradually extending it, and finish with the prayer.

The new series of books for children is Jenny Dent's *Spiritual Teaching for Children.* [1] The four initial titles in this series are: *God Loves Us All; Where is Heaven?; The Giant Jigsaw* and *The Great Teachers*. All pages have black-and-white illustrations designed for children to colour. There are also project pages which can be cut out and used separately by young children, which prevents them from scribbling over the entire book!

I cannot omit to mention Joan Hodgson's splendid *Hello Sun*, which is a firm favourite with so many families. It is presented in a delightful way to children aged three to eight and deals with the things that matter — with life and with our Creator — and also her *Our Father*, which has prayers and meditations for young children and is centred around the Lord's prayer. [2]

References

Introduction
1. The first book about the teaching of White Eagle, *Thy Kingdom Come* by Ivan Cooke, was published in 1932.

Chapter 1
1. Ivan Cooke (ed) *The Return of Sir Arthur Conan Doyle* (White Eagle Publishing Trust, 1956).
2. White Eagle, *The Living Word of St. John* (White Eagle Publishing Trust, 1949).
3. *ibid.*

Chapter 2
1. Grace Cooke, *Who is White Eagle?* (White Eagle Publishing Trust, 1969).
2. Grace Cooke, *The Illumined Ones* (White Eagle Publishing Trust, 1966).
3. Grace Cooke, *Sun Men of the Americas* (White Eagle Publishing Trust, 1975).
4. Joan Hodgson, *Planetary Harmonies* (White Eagle Publishing Trust, 1981) Chapter 2.
5. Jenny Dent, *Great Teachers* (White Eagle Publishing Trust, 1982).
6. White Eagle, leaflet *The White Eagle Brotherhood* (White Eagle Publishing Trust, 1969).
7. Joan Hodgson, *Why on Earth* (White Eagle Publishing Trust, 1964).

8. Cynthia, the Lady Sandys, *The Awakening Letters* (Neville Spearman, 1978).

Chapter 3
1. Hodgson, *Why on Earth*.
2. Grace Cooke, *Meditation, The New Mediumship* and *The Jewel in the Lotus* (White Eagle Publishing Trust, 1955, 1965 and 1973).
3. Leaflet *Spiritual Communion* (White Eagle Publishing Trust, 1970).
4. Cooke, *Meditation*, p. 14.
5. Cooke, *Meditation*.
6. Joan Hodgson in *Stella Polaris*, October/November, 1982.

Chapter 4
1. White Eagle, *The Quiet Mind* (White Eagle Publishing Trust, 1972).

Appendix B
1. Alice Bailey, *Esoteric Astrology* (Lucis Press, 1951).
2. A. G. S. Norris, *Transcendental Astrology* (Rider 1971).

Appendix C
1. *Spriritual Teaching for Children series* (White Eagle Publishing Trust, 1982).
2. Joan Hodgson, *Hullo Sun* (White Eagle Publishing Trust, 1977).

Details of White Eagle Lodges and Groups

White Eagle Groups in Great Britain and Ireland
At time of going to press and in alphabetical order:

Aberdeen area (Aboyne)
Acton

Bath
Bedfont
Berkhamsted
Birchington
Bradford
Bridport
Brighton
Bristol
Broadstairs
Bromley
Burley
Bury St. Edmunds

Camberley
Clacton
Congleton
Cromer
Croydon

Derby
Dover

Eastbourne

Falmouth
Felixstowe
Freshwater (Isle of Wight)

Glasgow
Glaslough
Gloucester
Guernsey (Channel Islands)

Hastings and St. Leonards
Hendon
High Barnet
Hornchurch
Hull

Ightham

Leeds
Leigh on Sea
Letchworth
Liphook
Lymington

Newcastle
Newport (Isle of Wight)
Norwich
North Cheam

Ossett

Peterborough
Preston

Rosemarkie
Ryedale

Saffron Walden
St. Albans
St. Leonards
Salisbury
Scarborough

Sheffield
Sidmouth
Southampton
Southport
Stanmore
Stockport
Stowmarket

Tewin
Tunbridge Wells

Uttoxeter
Uxbridge

Willerby (Hull)
Winscombe
Wirral
Woodbridge

Overseas Groups

Holland	The Hague, Ede
Sweden	Stockholm (Johanneshov), Eskilstuna, Gothenburg, Jönköping, Linköping, Orebro, Halmstad
Norway	Odnes
Switzerland	Lausanne, Zurich
Italy	Florence
Denmark	Copenhagen (Hvidovre)
Germany	Munich
Malta	Senglea
Australia	Melbourne, Sydney, Falconbridge, Perth
Canada	Mississauga, Stony Creek, Toronto, Ile Bizard, Vancouver
USA	Brainerd (Minn), Dallas (Tx), Houston (Tx), Lake Montezuma (Az), Long Beach (Ca), Monroe (Conn), Phoenix (Az), Pleasantville (NJ), San Francisco (Menlo Park, Ca), Scottsdale (Az), Tempe (Az)
Mexico	Mexico City
Brazil	Rio de Janeiro

Ghana	Accra, Nsawan, Takoradi
Nigeria	Lagos, Port Harcourt, Ibadan, Enugu
South Africa	Cape Town, Betty's Bay, Durban, Johannesburg

White Eagle Lodges
New Lands, Rake, Liss, Hants.
London
Edinburgh
Ipswich
Reading
East Sussex
Bournemouth
Teignmouth
Plymouth
Brisbane (Australia)